BEYOND HIS BARRIERS

WOMEN THRIVING IN MALE-DOMINATED FIELDS

DR. MINAKSHI BANSAL

DEDICATION

To the trailblazers, the glass ceiling shatterers, the women who dared to dream and defied expectations.

To the mentors, the allies, and the champions of change, who paved the way for others to follow.

And to the next generation of women leaders, who will continue to break barriers and build a more equitable world.

May this book inspire you to unleash your full potential and create your own path to success.

ᚦᚦᚦ

Contents

Contents

Contents

Prayer

"Om Bhadram Karnebhih Shrinuyama Devah

Bhadram Pashyemakshabhiryajatrah

Sthirairangais Tushtuvamsastanubhih

Vyashema Devahitam Yadayuh

Svasti Na Indro Vriddhashravah

Svasti Nah Pusha Vishwavedah

Svasti Nastarkshyo Arishtanemih

Svasti No Brihaspatir Dadhatu

Om Shantih Shantih Shantih"

This mantra is a prayer for universal well-being, invoking the blessings of various deities for protection, health, and happiness. It emphasizes the importance of experiencing the auspicious through all senses and living a life aligned with divine purpose. The repetition of "Shantih" at the end signifies a deep desire for peace in the individual, the environment, and the universe at large. This mantra is often recited as a prayer for peace, prosperity, and the physical and spiritual well-being of all beings.

ᗡᗡᗡ

About The Author

This book represents the culmination of extensive research and meticulous analysis, incorporating a diverse range of sources, including numerous books, scholarly studies, and personal experiences. Additionally, I have scoured various websites to gather relevant information and data essential for the compilation of this work. I have taken every precaution to ensure the accuracy of the information presented and have diligently cited all sources to acknowledge their contributions.

From her earliest days, Minakshi was distinguished by an insatiable appetite for reading. Her literary universe was inhabited by characters and narratives that spanned ethical tales, motivational and inspirational stories, and the mythic parables imbued with life lessons. This voracious reading habit was not merely for personal edification but was driven by a desire to distill and disseminate the essence of these narratives to foster the development of students and peers alike. She was particularly captivated by the lives and teachings of historical figures and spiritual leaders such as Adi Shankaracharya, Swami Vivekananda, Dr. APJ Abdul Kalam, Mahamana Pandit Madan Mohan Malviya, Mahatma Gandhi, Sardar Vallabhai Patel, and Vinoba Bhave, among others. Their philosophies and life stories fueled her ambition to embody their ideals of resilience, selflessness, and relentless pursuit of knowledge.

Dr. Minakshi's academic and practical engagement with psychology has been equally noteworthy. As a research scholar, her focus has been on exploring the intricate tapestry of the human psyche, aiming to unlock the potential for psychological well-being and societal harmony. Her scholarly work is complemented by her active involvement in social work, where she employs her academic insights to make tangible differences in the lives of the underprivileged. Her endeavours in social work are characterized by an innovative approach that combines traditional wisdom with contemporary psychological practices to address the multifaceted challenges faced by these communities.

Her artistic talents, another facet of her diverse capabilities, are not merely a personal passion but also serve as a medium through which she communicates and connects with others. Her art, rich in symbolism and emotional depth, reflects her philosophical inquiries and social concerns, offering viewers a glimpse into the breadth of her intellect and the depth of her compassion.

In addition to her contributions to the arts and social sciences, Dr. Minakshi has embraced the healing arts of Pranic Healing, mastering the techniques developed by Master Choa Kok Sui. This practice, which focuses on the manipulation of Prana or life energy to heal the body and aura, has been both a personal journey of discovery and a means through which she extends her healing touch to others. Her proficiency in Pranic Healing is complemented by her advocacy and teaching of various forms of meditation aimed at rejuvenation, personal betterment, and the cultivation of harmony within individuals and communities alike.

Dr. Minakshi's life is a narrative of relentless pursuit, not just of personal achievement but of the upliftment and empowerment of society at large. Her diverse interests and talents—spanning the arts, literature, psychology, and the healing practices—converge on a singular path of service. She embodies the spirit of the luminaries who inspired her, channelling their legacy through her actions and teachings. Through her books, art, and social initiatives, she continues to inspire a new generation to embark on their own journeys of self-discovery, resilience, and altruism.

Her commitment to social betterment, particularly her focus on uplifting underprivileged children, reflects a deep understanding of the transformative potential of education and personal development. By integrating her knowledge of psychology, her artistic sensibilities, and her healing practices, Dr. Bansal has developed a holistic approach to social work that addresses both the immediate needs and the long-term well-being of the communities she serves.

As an author, Dr. Minakshi's writings offer a blend of inspirational insights, practical wisdom, and reflective contemplations drawn from her extensive reading and life experiences. Her books serve as a guide for those seeking to navigate the complexities of life with grace, resilience, and purpose. Through her narratives, she extends an invitation to her readers to explore the depths of their own potential and to contribute meaningfully to the collective well-being of society.

In Dr. Minakshi Bansal, we find a remarkable synthesis of the artist, the scholar, the healer, and the social activist. Her life's work stands as a beacon of hope and a source of inspiration for individuals seeking to make a difference in the world. Her story is a compelling reminder of the power of individual action, rooted in compassion and driven by a profound commitment to the betterment of humanity. Dr. Minakshi's legacy is not just in the tangible outcomes of her efforts but in the enduring spirit of inquiry, empathy, and service that she embodies.

❦❦❦

Preface

In the tapestry of human history, women have consistently demonstrated resilience, ingenuity, and unwavering determination to break down barriers and shatter glass ceilings. "Beyond His Barriers: Women Thriving in Male-Dominated Fields" is a testament to this indomitable spirit, showcasing the extraordinary journeys of women who have not only survived but thrived in industries traditionally dominated by men.

As a woman who has navigated the complexities and challenges of these fields, I have witnessed firsthand the grit and grace required to not only gain a foothold but to excel and leave an enduring mark. This book is born from a deep desire to celebrate these pioneers, to amplify their voices, and to inspire future generations of women to pursue their passions with unwavering conviction.

Within these pages, you will encounter stories of women from diverse backgrounds and industries, each a beacon of hope and possibility. From the boardroom to the construction site, the laboratory to the sports arena, these women have defied expectations, challenged stereotypes, and paved the way for others to follow.

This book is not simply a collection of individual narratives; it is a testament to the collective strength and resilience of women. It is an exploration of the unique challenges women face in male-dominated fields, as well as the innovative solutions they have devised to overcome them. It is a celebration of mentorship, sisterhood, and the power of lifting each other up.

My hope is that "Beyond His Barriers" will serve as a source of inspiration, guidance, and solidarity for women everywhere. May it ignite a fire within you to pursue your dreams, to challenge the status quo, and to break down any barriers that stand in your way. Remember, your potential is limitless, and your contributions to the world are invaluable.

To the trailblazers, the innovators, the game-changers: this book is for you. May your stories continue to inspire and empower women for generations to come.

With gratitude and admiration,

Dr. Minakshi Bansal
Social Activist
Ahmedabad, Gujarat, Bharat

❦❦❦

ONE

FIRST IN LINE: THE WOMEN WHO FORGED NEW PATHS

In the annals of history, women have always been present, their contributions often obscured or minimized. Yet, in the face of overwhelming odds, countless women have defied societal expectations, breaking barriers and forging new paths in traditionally male-dominated fields. Their stories are tales of resilience, determination, and unwavering belief in their own abilities.

Long before the term "glass ceiling" was coined, women were already pushing against invisible barriers. They faced discrimination, prejudice, and exclusion, yet they persevered. In the realm of science, women like Marie Curie defied gender norms and revolutionized our understanding of radioactivity, earning her not one, but two Nobel Prizes. Her groundbreaking research paved the way for countless discoveries in physics and medicine.

In the world of aviation, Amelia Earhart became a symbol of female empowerment, soaring through the skies at a time when women were barely allowed behind the wheel of a car. Her adventurous spirit and unwavering determination inspired generations of women to reach for their dreams, no matter how audacious.

In the political arena, women like Eleanor Roosevelt and Indira Gandhi shattered the mold of traditional First Ladies, becoming influential figures in their own right. They championed social justice, human rights, and equality, leaving an indelible mark on the world stage.

These trailblazing women were not merely exceptions to the rule; they were pioneers who paved the way for countless others. Their courage and tenacity opened doors that had long been closed to women. They challenged the status quo, proving that gender was no barrier to achievement.

The struggle for equality in male-dominated fields has been a long and arduous one. Women have had to fight for their right to be taken seriously, to be heard, and to be respected. They have had to overcome stereotypes and prejudices that have been deeply ingrained in society for centuries.

Yet, despite these challenges, women have continued to rise. They have excelled in every field imaginable, from medicine and law to engineering and business. They have become CEOs, astronauts, scientists, artists, and athletes. They have broken records, won awards, and made history.

The stories of these women are not just inspiring; they are essential. They show us what is possible when we refuse to be limited by societal expectations. They remind us that we are capable of achieving great things, no matter our gender.

These women are role models for future generations. They teach us the importance of perseverance, resilience, and self-belief. They show us that we can overcome any obstacle if we set our minds to it.

The fight for gender equality is far from over. Women still face discrimination and inequality in many areas of life. But the progress that has been made is undeniable. Thanks to the trailblazing women who came before us, the world is a more equitable place for women today.

We owe a debt of gratitude to these pioneers. They have shown us the way, and it is up to us to continue their legacy. We must continue to fight for equality, to break down barriers, and to create a world where all women have the opportunity to reach their full potential.

The women who forged new paths in male-dominated fields are not just heroes; they are beacons of hope. They remind us that anything is possible when we dare to dream big and work hard to achieve our goals. Their stories are a testament to the power of the human spirit, and they will continue to inspire generations to come.

ᗪᗪᗪ

"She didn't just break the glass ceiling; she shattered it, showering the world with a kaleidoscope of possibilities."

In a realm dominated by men, she rose not as an exception, but as a testament to a woman's unwavering spirit. Her path is a beacon, guiding generations to defy expectations and claim their rightful place.

TWO
DEFYING EXPECTATIONS: STORIES OF RESILIENCE AND DETERMINATION

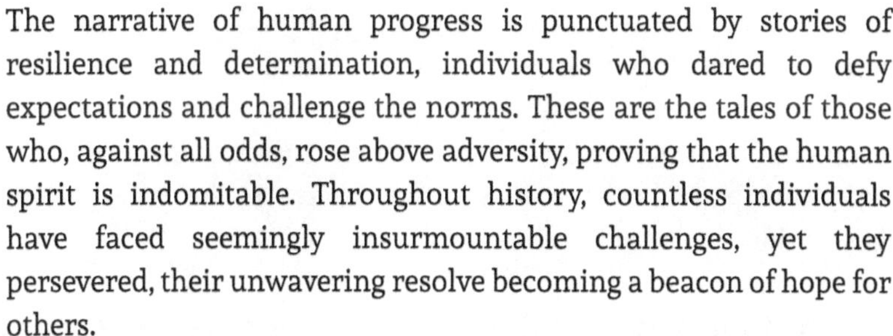

The narrative of human progress is punctuated by stories of resilience and determination, individuals who dared to defy expectations and challenge the norms. These are the tales of those who, against all odds, rose above adversity, proving that the human spirit is indomitable. Throughout history, countless individuals have faced seemingly insurmountable challenges, yet they persevered, their unwavering resolve becoming a beacon of hope for others.

Consider the story of Malala Yousafzai, the Pakistani activist who, at a young age, stood up against the Taliban's ban on girls' education. Despite facing death threats and an assassination attempt, Malala's determination to champion the right to education for all children remained unyielding. Her courage and resilience inspired a global movement and earned her the Nobel Peace Prize, making her the youngest recipient in history.

The world of sports has also witnessed remarkable displays of resilience. Wilma Rudolph, an American athlete, overcame childhood polio and a diagnosis of being unable to walk again to become a three-time Olympic gold medalist in track and field. Her story is a testament to the power of perseverance and the ability of the human spirit to overcome physical limitations.

In the realm of science and innovation, Stephen Hawking defied medical expectations. Diagnosed with amyotrophic lateral sclerosis (ALS) at the age of 21, Hawking was given a life expectancy of a few years. However, he went on to live a full and productive life, revolutionizing our understanding of the universe with his groundbreaking theories on black holes and the origins of the cosmos. His life story is a powerful reminder that the human mind is capable of extraordinary feats, even in the face of physical challenges.

Resilience is not solely the domain of individuals; it is also a defining characteristic of communities and nations. The story of Japan's recovery after World War II is a testament to the collective resilience of a people. Despite facing immense devastation and loss, the Japanese people rebuilt their nation, transforming it into an economic powerhouse and a global leader in technology and innovation.

In recent times, the COVID-19 pandemic has presented a global challenge that has tested the resilience of individuals, communities, and healthcare systems worldwide. Yet, amidst the suffering and loss, stories of courage and determination have emerged. Healthcare workers on the frontlines, risking their lives to save others, have become symbols of hope and resilience. Communities have come together to support one another, demonstrating the power of human connection in times of crisis.

These stories of resilience and determination remind us that adversity is not the end, but rather an opportunity for growth and transformation. They teach us that setbacks and failures are not permanent, but rather stepping stones on the path to success. They inspire us to embrace challenges, to persevere in the face of adversity, and to never give up on our dreams.

The importance of resilience in navigating life's challenges cannot be overstated. It is the ability to bounce back from setbacks, to adapt to change, and to find strength in adversity. Resilience is not about avoiding pain or difficulty, but rather about finding ways to cope with and overcome them.

Cultivating resilience is a lifelong journey. It involves developing a positive mindset, building strong social connections, learning from failures, and taking care of our physical and mental health. It is about recognizing our own strengths and weaknesses, and finding ways to leverage our strengths and overcome our weaknesses.

In a world that is constantly changing and presenting new challenges, resilience is an essential life skill. It is the key to thriving in the face of adversity, to achieving our goals, and to living a fulfilling life. The stories of those who have defied expectations and overcome challenges serve as a constant reminder that the human spirit is resilient, and that with determination and perseverance, we can overcome any obstacle.

The tales of resilience and determination are not merely stories of individual triumph; they are a reflection of the human spirit's ability to adapt, overcome, and thrive. They inspire us to embrace challenges, to persevere in the face of adversity, and to never give up on our dreams. They remind us that we are capable of extraordinary feats, and that our potential is limitless.

❦❦❦

"Resilience is not the absence of fear, but the triumph over it."

In the face of adversity, she found strength within herself, her spirit unyielding like a diamond forged under pressure. Her journey is a testament that every challenge is an opportunity for growth and transformation.

THREE

Breaking the Mold: Challenging Gender Stereotypes in the Workplace

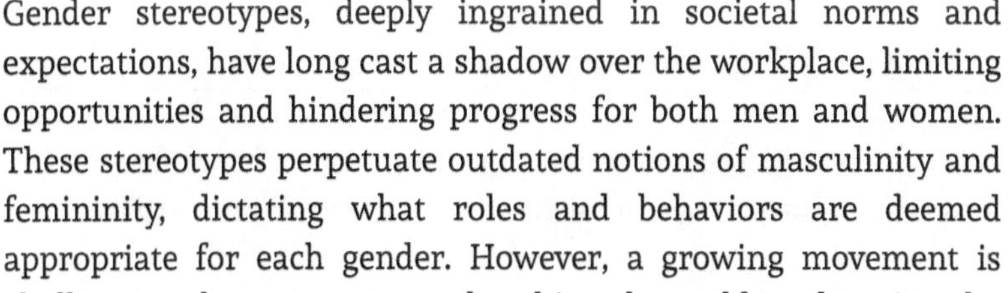

Gender stereotypes, deeply ingrained in societal norms and expectations, have long cast a shadow over the workplace, limiting opportunities and hindering progress for both men and women. These stereotypes perpetuate outdated notions of masculinity and femininity, dictating what roles and behaviors are deemed appropriate for each gender. However, a growing movement is challenging these stereotypes, breaking the mold, and paving the way for a more inclusive and equitable workplace.

The consequences of gender stereotypes in the workplace are far-reaching. For women, these stereotypes often lead to being underestimated and undervalued. They may be perceived as less competent or assertive than their male counterparts, leading to missed opportunities for promotions and leadership roles. Women in traditionally male-dominated fields, such as STEM, may face additional barriers due to biases and assumptions about their abilities.

Men, too, are affected by gender stereotypes. They may feel pressured to conform to traditional notions of masculinity, suppressing emotions or interests that are deemed "unmanly." This can lead to stress, burnout, and a lack of authenticity in the workplace. Additionally, men who choose to pursue careers in traditionally female-dominated fields, such as nursing or teaching, may face stigma and discrimination.

Breaking the mold of gender stereotypes requires a multifaceted approach. One crucial step is raising awareness and challenging unconscious biases. Many individuals hold implicit biases that they are not even aware of, and these biases can influence decision-making in the workplace. By educating employees about unconscious bias and providing training on how to mitigate its effects, organizations can create a more inclusive environment.

Another important aspect of breaking the mold is promoting diversity and inclusion. This means creating a workplace culture where individuals of all genders, races, ethnicities, sexual orientations, and abilities feel valued and respected. It also means ensuring that hiring and promotion practices are fair and equitable, and that opportunities for advancement are available to all.

Mentorship and sponsorship programs can also play a vital role in breaking down gender stereotypes. By connecting women and underrepresented groups with experienced mentors and sponsors, organizations can provide valuable guidance and support, helping individuals navigate the challenges of the workplace and reach their full potential.

Flexible work arrangements can also contribute to a more inclusive workplace. By offering options such as telecommuting, flexible hours, and job sharing, organizations can accommodate the diverse needs of their employees, including those with caregiving responsibilities. This can help to level the playing field for women and other groups who may face challenges balancing work and family life.

In addition to these organizational efforts, individuals can also play a role in challenging gender stereotypes. By speaking up against discriminatory behavior, advocating for themselves and others, and challenging assumptions about gender roles, individuals can help to create a more inclusive workplace culture.

The benefits of breaking the mold of gender stereotypes are numerous. For individuals, it means having the freedom to pursue their passions and talents without being limited by societal expectations. It means being valued for their contributions, regardless of their gender.

For organizations, breaking the mold can lead to increased innovation, creativity, and productivity. By tapping into the diverse perspectives and experiences of their employees, organizations can gain a competitive advantage and better serve their customers.

A more inclusive workplace also benefits society as a whole. By breaking down gender stereotypes, we can create a more equitable world where everyone has the opportunity to reach their full potential.

The journey to break the mold of gender stereotypes is ongoing, but significant progress has been made. More and more women are entering leadership roles, and organizations are recognizing the importance of diversity and inclusion. However, there is still much work to be done.

By continuing to challenge unconscious biases, promote diversity and inclusion, and support flexible work arrangements, we can create a workplace where gender stereotypes are a thing of the past. It is a future worth striving for, where everyone can thrive, regardless of their gender.

 PPP

"She challenged the mold, refusing to be confined by stereotypes."

She dared to dream differently, to carve a path uncharted, her spirit a testament to the power of individuality. Her legacy is a blueprint for every woman to redefine success on her own terms.

FOUR

Navigating the Labyrinth: Overcoming Bias and Discrimination

The path to success in any field is rarely a straight line, but for women in male-dominated arenas, it often resembles a labyrinth fraught with hidden biases and overt discrimination. These obstacles can be demoralizing and disenfranchising, but they are not insurmountable. Navigating this labyrinth requires a blend of resilience, strategic thinking, and unwavering self-belief.

Bias, often unconscious and deeply ingrained, can manifest in subtle ways that create an uneven playing field. Microaggressions, such as being interrupted or having ideas dismissed, can chip away at confidence and create a hostile environment. Studies have shown that women are more likely to be evaluated based on their personality traits rather than their accomplishments, while men are often given the benefit of the doubt. This can lead to women being overlooked for promotions and leadership roles, even when they are equally or more qualified than their male counterparts.

Discrimination, on the other hand, is often more overt and can take many forms, from unequal pay and limited opportunities to outright harassment. It can be a demoralizing experience, leaving women feeling isolated and undervalued. However, it is crucial to remember that discrimination is illegal and should never be tolerated.

Overcoming bias and discrimination requires a multi-pronged approach. First and foremost, it is essential to recognize and acknowledge that these issues exist. Many people are unaware of their own biases or the impact they can have on others. By educating ourselves and others about unconscious bias, we can take steps to mitigate its effects.

Building a strong support network is also crucial. This can include mentors, sponsors, colleagues, friends, and family members who can offer guidance, encouragement, and a safe space to vent frustrations. Networking with other women in similar fields can also be invaluable, providing a sense of community and shared experience.

Developing resilience is another key factor in navigating the labyrinth of bias and discrimination. This means learning to bounce back from setbacks, maintaining a positive attitude, and focusing on one's goals. It also means developing coping mechanisms for dealing with stress and adversity.

Self-advocacy is also essential. Women must be willing to speak up for themselves, to negotiate for fair pay and opportunities, and to challenge discriminatory behavior. This can be intimidating, but it is necessary to create a more equitable workplace.

Organizations also have a role to play in combating bias and discrimination. They can implement diversity and inclusion training, establish clear policies against discrimination, and create a culture of respect and fairness. They can also provide resources and support for employees who experience discrimination.

Legal action may also be necessary in some cases. If discrimination is suspected, it is important to document the incidents and seek advice from a legal professional. There are laws in place to protect against discrimination, and it is important to hold employers accountable for creating a safe and equitable workplace.

The journey to overcome bias and discrimination is not an easy one, but it is a necessary one. By working together, we can create a world where everyone has the opportunity to thrive, regardless of their gender. This requires a collective effort from individuals, organizations, and society as a whole.

We must continue to challenge stereotypes, advocate for ourselves and others, and work to create a more inclusive and equitable workplace. By doing so, we can dismantle the labyrinth of bias and discrimination, paving the way for a brighter future for all. The path may be winding and fraught with challenges, but with determination, resilience, and unwavering self-belief, we can emerge victorious, having forged a new path for ourselves and for generations to come.

ϼϼϼ

"Navigating the labyrinth of bias, she emerged as a
beacon of hope."

With unwavering determination, she transformed
obstacles into stepping stones, her journey
illuminating the path for others. Her story is a
testament to the power of perseverance and the
pursuit of equity.

FIVE

MENTORSHIP MATTERS: THE POWER OF FEMALE ROLE MODELS

In the tapestry of human development, role models serve as guiding lights, illuminating paths towards success and fulfillment. For women navigating male-dominated fields, the power of female role models is particularly profound. These mentors offer more than just advice; they provide a blueprint for navigating challenges, a source of inspiration, and a testament to what is possible.

The significance of mentorship stems from its ability to foster personal and professional growth. Mentors provide a safe space for mentees to share their aspirations, fears, and vulnerabilities. They offer guidance based on their own experiences, helping mentees navigate the complexities of their chosen fields. This guidance can be instrumental in helping women overcome self-doubt, develop confidence, and make informed decisions about their careers.

For women in male-dominated fields, female role models offer a unique form of representation and understanding. They have walked similar paths, faced similar challenges, and emerged victorious. Their stories of resilience, determination, and success serve as a beacon of hope, demonstrating that it is possible to break barriers and thrive in environments where women are often underrepresented.

Female mentors also provide invaluable insights into the unwritten rules of the workplace. They can share strategies for navigating office politics, building relationships with colleagues, and advocating for oneself. This knowledge can be particularly crucial for women, who may face subtle biases and discrimination that can hinder their progress.

The impact of female role models extends beyond the workplace. They can inspire women to pursue their passions, challenge societal expectations, and embrace their unique strengths. They can encourage women to take risks, to speak up, and to lead with confidence.

Research has shown that having a mentor can significantly impact a woman's career trajectory. Mentees are more likely to be promoted, earn higher salaries, and report greater job satisfaction. They are also more likely to stay in their chosen fields, contributing to a more diverse and inclusive workforce.

The power of female role models is not limited to formal mentorship programs. It can also be found in the stories of women who have achieved success in their chosen fields. These stories, whether shared through books, articles, or social media, can inspire and motivate women to pursue their own dreams.

The rise of women in leadership positions across various sectors is a testament to the power of mentorship. Women who have benefited from mentorship are now paying it forward, mentoring the next generation of female leaders. This creates a virtuous cycle, where the success of one woman empowers and inspires countless others.

While the power of female role models is undeniable, it is important to acknowledge that mentorship is not a one-size-fits-all solution. The most effective mentorship relationships are built on trust, mutual respect, and a shared commitment to growth. It is also important to recognize that not all women will have access to formal mentorship programs or the opportunity to connect with successful women in their fields.

However, the power of role models can still be harnessed through other means. Women can seek out mentors in different fields, or even in different stages of their careers. They can also find inspiration and guidance from fictional characters, historical figures, or even their own mothers and grandmothers.

The key is to actively seek out sources of inspiration and support. By surrounding themselves with positive role models, women can cultivate the confidence, resilience, and determination needed to overcome challenges and achieve their goals.

In conclusion, the power of female role models is undeniable. They provide guidance, inspiration, and a roadmap for success. They empower women to break barriers, challenge stereotypes, and reach their full potential. By investing in mentorship and celebrating the achievements of women in all fields, we can create a more equitable and inclusive world, where every woman has the opportunity to thrive.

ϷϷϷ

"In the symphony of voices, she found her melody."

Amidst the chorus of doubt, she discovered her strength, her voice ringing true with authenticity. Her journey is a testament to the power of self-belief and the courage to speak one's truth.

SIX

FINDING YOUR VOICE: SPEAKING UP AND ADVOCATING FOR YOURSELF

In a world that often tries to silence or diminish individual voices, finding one's own and using it to advocate for oneself is a powerful act of self-empowerment. This is especially true for women navigating male-dominated fields, where their perspectives and contributions may be overlooked or undervalued. Finding your voice is not just about speaking up; it's about asserting your worth, claiming your space, and shaping your own narrative.

The journey to finding your voice begins with self-awareness. It requires understanding your values, beliefs, and passions. What are the issues that matter most to you? What are your strengths and weaknesses? What are your goals and aspirations? By gaining clarity on these questions, you can start to articulate your thoughts and feelings with confidence and conviction.

One of the biggest obstacles to finding your voice is fear. Fear of judgment, rejection, or retaliation can hold us back from speaking up. However, it's important to remember that your voice matters. Your perspective is valuable, and your contributions are worthy of recognition. By acknowledging and addressing your fears, you can start to overcome them and find the courage to speak your truth.

Developing your voice also involves honing your communication skills. This means learning how to express yourself clearly, concisely, and persuasively. It also means learning how to listen actively, to understand different perspectives, and to find common ground. Effective communication is essential for advocating for yourself and your ideas.

Finding your voice is not a one-time event; it's an ongoing process. It requires practice, patience, and perseverance. Start by speaking up in small ways, such as sharing your ideas in a meeting or offering feedback to a colleague. As you gain confidence, you can gradually take on bigger challenges, such as advocating for a raise or promotion, or speaking out against injustice or inequality.

It's important to remember that finding your voice is not just about speaking up for yourself; it's also about advocating for others. By using your voice to amplify the voices of those who are marginalized or silenced, you can contribute to a more inclusive and equitable world.

One of the most powerful ways to find your voice is to surround yourself with supportive people. Seek out mentors, colleagues, friends, and family members who believe in you and encourage you to speak your mind. Join networks or communities of like-minded individuals who share your values and interests. These connections can provide a safe space for you to explore your ideas and develop your voice.

Another important aspect of finding your voice is self-care. Taking care of your physical and mental health is essential for maintaining your energy and resilience. Make sure you are getting enough sleep, eating a healthy diet, exercising regularly, and engaging in activities that bring you joy. When you are well-rested and energized, you are more likely to feel confident and empowered to speak up.

Finding your voice is not always easy, but it is always worth it. By speaking up and advocating for yourself, you can create positive change in your own life and in the world around you. You can inspire others to find their own voices and to speak their truth. Remember, your voice is a powerful tool. Use it wisely, and use it well.

"Building bridges, not barriers, she created a network of empowerment."

With a heart full of compassion and a vision for a better future, she fostered a community of support. Her legacy is a testament to the power of collaboration and the strength found in unity.

SEVEN

BUILDING NETWORKS: CREATING COMMUNITIES OF SUPPORT

In the intricate dance of personal and professional growth, the value of robust networks cannot be overstated. For women navigating male-dominated fields, these networks are not just beneficial; they are essential. They serve as pillars of strength, offering guidance, resources, and a sense of belonging in landscapes that can often feel isolating.

The intentional act of building networks, of creating communities of support, is a powerful strategy for women to thrive and succeed in their chosen fields.

At its core, a network is a web of connections that link individuals with shared interests, goals, or experiences. These connections can be formal or informal, professional or personal, but they all contribute to a sense of community and shared purpose.

For women in male-dominated fields, these networks can provide a safe space to share challenges, celebrate successes, and gain insights from those who have walked similar paths.

Building a network is a proactive process that requires intentionality and effort. It involves identifying individuals who can offer support and guidance, reaching out to them, and cultivating meaningful relationships.

This can be done through attending industry events, joining professional organizations, participating in online communities, or simply connecting with colleagues and peers.

The benefits of building networks are numerous. Firstly, networks provide access to information and resources that may not be readily available otherwise. This can include job opportunities, industry trends, professional development resources, and even emotional support.

By tapping into the collective knowledge and experience of their network, women can gain a competitive edge and accelerate their career growth.

Secondly, networks offer a platform for collaboration and mutual support. By connecting with others who share similar goals and challenges, women can build relationships that are both personally and professionally rewarding.

They can collaborate on projects, share ideas, and offer each other support and encouragement. This sense of community can be particularly valuable in male-dominated fields, where women may feel isolated or marginalized.

Thirdly, networks can help women develop their leadership skills and confidence. By interacting with successful individuals and observing their leadership styles, women can gain valuable insights and learn from their experiences. They can also find mentors who can provide guidance and support as they navigate their careers.

Building networks is not just about individual gain; it is also about creating a more inclusive and equitable workplace. By supporting and empowering each other, women can challenge the status quo and create a more welcoming environment for future generations. This can involve advocating for policies that support women's advancement, mentoring younger women, and amplifying each other's voices.

Creating communities of support is an essential aspect of building networks. These communities can take many forms, from formal organizations to informal groups of friends and colleagues.

They provide a safe space for women to share their experiences, seek advice, and celebrate their achievements. They also offer opportunities for networking, mentorship, and professional development.

The power of community is undeniable. It provides a sense of belonging, a support system, and a platform for collective action. By coming together, women can amplify their voices, advocate for change, and create a more equitable and inclusive world.

The act of building networks and creating communities of support is an investment in oneself and in the future of women in male-dominated fields. It is a testament to the resilience, determination, and ambition of women who refuse to be limited by societal expectations.

By forging connections, sharing knowledge, and supporting each other, women can break barriers, achieve their goals, and pave the way for future generations.

In a world that is constantly evolving, the ability to build and maintain strong networks is more important than ever. It is a skill that can be learned and honed over time.

By being proactive, intentional, and genuine in their approach, women can create networks that will serve them throughout their careers and beyond. The power of connection is transformative, and it is a power that women can harness to achieve extraordinary things.

ppp

"In the delicate dance of life, she found harmony
between ambition and love."

With grace and resilience, she navigated the
complexities of career and family, her journey an
inspiration to women juggling multiple roles. Her
story is a testament to the power of balance and the
pursuit of a fulfilling life.

EIGHT

Balancing Act: Juggling Career and Personal Life

The modern world often presents a relentless juggling act, particularly for women striving to excel in their careers while maintaining a fulfilling personal life. This balancing act becomes even more intricate for women in male-dominated fields, where the demands and expectations can be particularly intense. However, achieving this balance is not only possible but also essential for overall well-being and sustained success.

The pursuit of a thriving career often demands significant time, energy, and dedication. For women in male-dominated fields, this can be amplified by the need to prove themselves and overcome biases. Long hours, demanding projects, and the pressure to constantly exceed expectations can leave little room for personal pursuits, relationships, and self-care.

On the other hand, neglecting one's personal life can lead to burnout, resentment, and a loss of passion for one's career. Nurturing relationships, pursuing hobbies, and taking time for relaxation and rejuvenation are essential for maintaining physical and mental well-being. It is in these moments of personal fulfillment that we find the energy and inspiration to excel in our professional lives.

The key to juggling career and personal life lies in finding a balance that works for each individual. There is no one-size-fits-all solution, as everyone's priorities, circumstances, and values are different. However, there are several strategies that can help women navigate this delicate balancing act.

Setting clear boundaries between work and personal life is crucial. This means establishing specific times for work and personal activities, and sticking to them as much as possible. It also means learning to say no to additional work commitments when necessary, and delegating tasks whenever possible.

Prioritizing self-care is another essential aspect of maintaining balance. This means making time for activities that promote physical and mental well-being, such as exercise, healthy eating, sleep, and relaxation techniques. It also means nurturing relationships with loved ones, pursuing hobbies and interests, and taking time for oneself.

Embracing flexibility is key in today's fast-paced world. This means being willing to adjust your schedule and priorities as needed. It also means being open to exploring alternative work arrangements, such as telecommuting or flexible hours, if they are available and alin with your goals.

Building a strong support system is invaluable for women juggling career and personal life. This can include family, friends, colleagues, mentors, and even professional coaches or therapists. These individuals can offer emotional support, practical advice, and a sounding board for ideas and concerns.

Setting realistic expectations is also important. It's easy to feel overwhelmed by the demands of both career and personal life, but it's important to remember that perfection is not the goal. Striving for progress, not perfection, can help alleviate stress and create a more sustainable balance.

Communicating your needs and expectations is crucial, both at work and at home. This means being clear about your priorities, boundaries, and limitations. It also means being willing to negotiate and compromise to find solutions that work for everyone involved.

Embracing technology can also be a helpful tool for managing the juggling act. There are numerous apps and tools available that can help with time management, organization, and communication. By leveraging these resources, women can streamline their tasks, reduce stress, and create more time for personal pursuits.

It's important to remember that the balancing act is an ongoing process. It requires constant reassessment and adjustment as life circumstances change. What works today may not work tomorrow, and that's okay. The key is to be adaptable, flexible, and willing to experiment to find what works best for you.

The journey to achieving a fulfilling career and personal life is not without its challenges, but the rewards are immeasurable. By prioritizing self-care, setting boundaries, embracing flexibility, building a strong support system, setting realistic expectations, communicating effectively, and leveraging technology, women can create a life that is both professionally rewarding and personally enriching. It is a balancing act that requires dedication and effort, but the payoff is a life that is truly balanced and fulfilling.

ᑭᑭᑭ

"Igniting the spark within, she empowered the next generation to lead."

With unwavering faith in the potential of young women, she nurtured their dreams and ignited their passion. Her legacy is a testament to the transformative power of mentorship and the ripple effect of inspiration.

NINE

EMPOWERING THE NEXT GENERATION: INSPIRING YOUNG WOMEN TO LEAD

Empowering the next generation of women to lead is not merely an act of goodwill; it is an imperative for a progressive and equitable society. The world is in dire need of diverse leadership that reflects the multifaceted nature of our global community. By inspiring and equipping young women with the tools and confidence to lead, we unlock a wellspring of untapped potential, paving the way for a more inclusive and prosperous future.

Leadership, in its truest form, is about inspiring and mobilizing others towards a common goal. It is about having the vision to see what is possible, the courage to challenge the status quo, and the ability to empower others to reach their full potential. Traditionally, leadership roles have been dominated by men, perpetuating a narrow and often exclusionary perspective. However, the rise of women in leadership positions across various sectors is challenging this paradigm, demonstrating the immense value that diverse perspectives bring to decision-making and problem-solving.

Young women today are growing up in a world that is more interconnected and complex than ever before. They are facing unprecedented challenges, from climate change to social inequality to political instability. To navigate this complex landscape, they need leadership skills that go beyond traditional models. They need to be equipped with critical thinking, creativity, collaboration, and resilience.

Empowering young women to lead starts with instilling in them a sense of self-belief and agency. This means challenging societal expectations and stereotypes that limit their aspirations. It means providing them with opportunities to explore their interests, develop their talents, and build their confidence.

Mentorship plays a crucial role in empowering young women to lead. By connecting them with successful women who have navigated similar paths, young women can gain invaluable insights, guidance, and support. Mentors can share their experiences, offer advice, and serve as role models, inspiring young women to reach for their dreams.

Education is another key pillar of empowerment. By providing young women with access to quality education, we equip them with the knowledge and skills they need to succeed. This includes not only academic subjects, but also leadership training, communication skills, and critical thinking. It also means creating learning environments that are inclusive, supportive, and empowering.

Exposure to diverse perspectives and experiences is also essential for developing well-rounded leaders. This can be achieved through travel, cultural exchange programs, and exposure to different viewpoints through literature, media, and the arts. By broadening their horizons, young women can gain a deeper understanding of the world and the challenges it faces.

Empowering young women to lead is not just about individual development; it is also about creating systemic change. This means challenging discriminatory practices and policies that hold women back. It means advocating for equal pay, representation in leadership positions, and opportunities for advancement. It also means creating a culture that values diversity, inclusion, and equity.

The benefits of empowering young women to lead are far-reaching. Studies have shown that companies with gender-diverse leadership teams are more innovative, profitable, and sustainable. They are also better equipped to address complex challenges and make decisions that reflect the needs of a diverse customer base.

Beyond the corporate world, women leaders are making a significant impact in politics, social activism, and community development. They are championing causes such as environmental protection, social justice, and education. Their leadership is essential for building a more equitable and sustainable world.

Empowering young women to lead is an investment in the future. It is about unleashing the potential of half the world's population and creating a more just and prosperous society for all. By providing young women with the tools, resources, and support they need to lead, we are not only empowering them as individuals, but we are also empowering the world.

The journey to empower the next generation of women to lead is ongoing, but the progress made so far is encouraging. More and more young women are stepping up and taking on leadership roles in various fields. Their voices are being heard, their ideas are being implemented, and their impact is being felt around the world.

By continuing to invest in mentorship, education, and systemic change, we can create a world where young women are not only empowered to lead, but where their leadership is celebrated and valued. It is a future worth striving for, where the full potential of humanity is unleashed, and where everyone has the opportunity to thrive.

ᗰᗰᗰ

*"Learning from the trailblazers, she ascended to
new heights."*

*Standing on the shoulders of giants, she embraced
their wisdom and carved her own path, her journey
a testament to the power of continuous learning
and growth. Her story is an ode to the leaders who
came before and the legacy she will leave behind.*

TEN

LESSONS FROM THE TOP: INSIGHTS FROM SUCCESSFUL WOMEN LEADERS

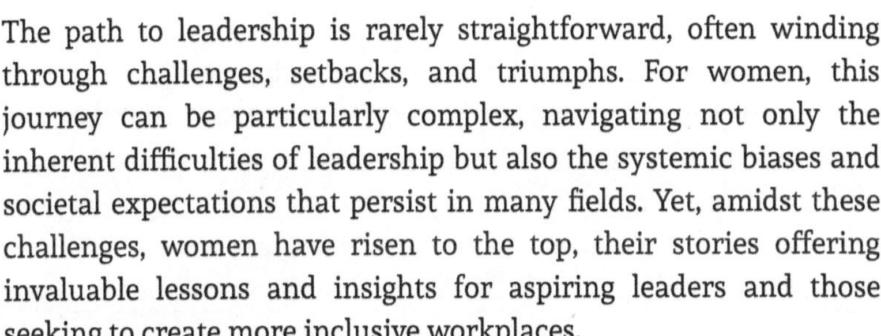

The path to leadership is rarely straightforward, often winding through challenges, setbacks, and triumphs. For women, this journey can be particularly complex, navigating not only the inherent difficulties of leadership but also the systemic biases and societal expectations that persist in many fields. Yet, amidst these challenges, women have risen to the top, their stories offering invaluable lessons and insights for aspiring leaders and those seeking to create more inclusive workplaces.

One of the most resonant lessons from successful women leaders is the importance of resilience. The ability to bounce back from setbacks, learn from failures, and persevere in the face of adversity is a hallmark of great leadership. Women leaders often share stories of overcoming discrimination, bias, and self-doubt, demonstrating that resilience is not just about surviving but thriving in the face of challenges. They emphasize the importance of developing a growth mindset, embracing challenges as opportunities for learning, and cultivating a strong support network to navigate difficult times.

Another key lesson is the power of authenticity. In a world that often pressures women to conform to certain molds, successful women leaders have shown the importance of staying true to oneself. They emphasize the need to embrace one's unique strengths, values, and leadership style. Authenticity not only fosters trust and respect from others but also allows leaders to connect with their teams on a deeper level, inspiring and motivating them to achieve shared goals.

The importance of building strong relationships and networks is another recurring theme in the stories of successful women leaders. They understand that leadership is not a solo act but a collaborative effort. They emphasize the value of mentorship, both as mentors and mentees, and the importance of building diverse and inclusive teams. They also recognize the power of collaboration, building alliances, and leveraging networks to achieve common goals.

Many successful women leaders also highlight the significance of continuous learning and development. They are constantly seeking new knowledge, skills, and experiences to expand their horizons and stay ahead of the curve. They invest in their own growth and encourage their teams to do the same. This commitment to lifelong learning not only enhances their leadership capabilities but also sets a positive example for their organizations.

Another important lesson is the need to advocate for oneself and others. Women leaders often face unique challenges in the workplace, such as being underestimated, interrupted, or having their ideas dismissed. They have learned to speak up, assert their authority, and advocate for their needs and the needs of their teams. They also champion diversity and inclusion, mentoring and sponsoring other women, and creating a more equitable workplace for all.

The stories of successful women leaders also reveal the importance of work-life balance, though the definition of balance may vary for each individual. They emphasize the need to set boundaries, prioritize self-care, and make time for family, friends, and personal interests. They recognize that a healthy work-life balance not only enhances their well-being but also makes them more effective leaders.

Finally, successful women leaders often speak of the importance of giving back to their communities and making a positive impact on the world. They use their platforms to advocate for social justice, environmental protection, and other causes they care about. They inspire others to use their talents and resources to make a difference, creating a ripple effect of positive change.

The insights gleaned from successful women leaders provide a roadmap for aspiring leaders, regardless of gender. They demonstrate the importance of resilience, authenticity, relationship building, continuous learning, self-advocacy, work-life balance, and giving back. By embracing these lessons, individuals can not only achieve their own leadership goals but also contribute to creating a more inclusive and equitable world where everyone has the opportunity to thrive.

ppp

"Diversity is not a checkbox; it's the vibrant tapestry of our shared humanity."

She celebrated differences, embracing a kaleidoscope of perspectives, her leadership a testament to the power of inclusion. Her journey is a blueprint for a world where every voice is valued and every story is heard.

ELEVEN

CHANGING THE GAME: STRATEGIES FOR CREATING A MORE INCLUSIVE WORKPLACE

The modern workplace is a dynamic, ever-evolving landscape, where diversity and inclusion are not just buzzwords but essential ingredients for success. A truly inclusive workplace fosters an environment where individuals from all backgrounds feel valued, respected, and empowered to contribute their unique perspectives and talents. This not only benefits the employees themselves but also drives innovation, creativity, and overall organizational performance. However, creating a more inclusive workplace requires a deliberate and strategic approach, one that involves changing the game at both the individual and organizational levels.

At the heart of creating an inclusive workplace is a shift in mindset. It requires moving beyond mere tolerance of diversity to embracing and celebrating it. This means recognizing that diversity encompasses not only race, gender, and ethnicity but also age, sexual orientation, disability, religion, socioeconomic status, and a wide range of other characteristics. It means acknowledging that each individual brings a unique perspective and set of experiences to the table, and that these differences are a source of strength, not weakness.

To foster this shift in mindset, organizations must invest in education and training on diversity and inclusion. This can include workshops, seminars, and online resources that help employees understand the importance of diversity, recognize their own biases, and develop skills for interacting with colleagues from different backgrounds. It is also important to create a culture of open dialogue and communication, where employees feel safe to share their experiences and perspectives.

Another key strategy for creating a more inclusive workplace is to ensure that diversity is reflected at all levels of the organization, from entry-level positions to the C-suite. This means implementing equitable hiring and promotion practices that give everyone a fair chance to succeed, regardless of their background. It also means providing mentorship and sponsorship programs to support the development of underrepresented groups.

In addition to representation, it is crucial to create an environment where everyone feels a sense of belonging. This means fostering a culture of respect and inclusivity, where all employees feel valued and heard. It also means providing opportunities for employees to connect with each other, both professionally and personally, through employee resource groups, social events, and other activities.

Inclusive leadership is another critical component of creating a more inclusive workplace. Leaders must model inclusive behavior, set clear expectations for their teams, and hold themselves and others accountable for creating a welcoming and respectful environment. They must also be willing to listen to feedback from employees and take action to address any concerns or issues that arise.

Flexible work arrangements can also contribute to a more inclusive workplace. By offering options such as telecommuting, flexible hours, and job sharing, organizations can accommodate the diverse needs of their employees, including those with caregiving responsibilities or disabilities. This can help to level the playing field and create a more equitable work environment.

Creating a more inclusive workplace is not a one-time effort but an ongoing process that requires continuous learning, adaptation, and commitment. It requires a willingness to challenge the status quo, to question assumptions, and to embrace change. It also requires a commitment to measuring progress and holding ourselves accountable for creating a workplace where everyone can thrive.

The benefits of creating a more inclusive workplace are significant. It can lead to increased innovation, creativity, and problem-solving, as diverse teams bring a wider range of perspectives and experiences to the table. It can also improve employee morale and engagement, as individuals feel valued and respected for who they are. Ultimately, creating a more inclusive workplace is not just the right thing to do; it is also the smart thing to do, as it can drive organizational success and create a more equitable and just society.

The journey to create a more inclusive workplace may not be easy, but it is a journey worth taking. By embracing diversity, challenging biases, and fostering a culture of inclusivity, we can change the game and create a workplace where everyone has the opportunity to thrive. It is a vision that requires courage, commitment, and collaboration, but the rewards are immeasurable. A more inclusive workplace is not just a goal; it is a necessity for a better future.

❦❦❦

*"A future where every girl dares to dream, to lead,
to change the world."*

*In her vision, she saw a world where gender is not a
barrier, but a catalyst for progress. Her legacy is a
commitment to empowering young women, to
fostering their leadership potential, and to creating
a more equitable future.*

TWELVE

From Imposter Syndrome to Confidence: Owning Your Accomplishments

Imposter syndrome, a pervasive and often debilitating phenomenon, can plague individuals across various fields and levels of achievement. It is the persistent feeling of being a fraud, of not deserving one's success, and the constant fear of being exposed as inadequate. This internalized doubt can be particularly pronounced for women in male-dominated fields, where societal expectations and biases can further exacerbate feelings of inadequacy. However, the journey from imposter syndrome to confidence is not only possible but also essential for personal and professional growth. It involves recognizing and challenging self-limiting beliefs, embracing one's accomplishments, and cultivating a mindset of self-worth and empowerment.

Imposter syndrome often stems from a complex interplay of factors, including perfectionism, fear of failure, and external validation. Perfectionists set unrealistically high standards for themselves, leading to a constant feeling of falling short. Fear of failure can paralyze individuals, preventing them from taking risks and pursuing their goals. The need for external validation can create a dependence on others' approval, leading to a lack of self-trust and confidence.

For women in male-dominated fields, imposter syndrome can be further fueled by societal expectations and biases. Women may feel pressure to constantly prove themselves, to be twice as good as their male counterparts to be taken seriously. They may also face microaggressions and subtle forms of discrimination that can chip away at their confidence and reinforce feelings of inadequacy.

The first step in overcoming imposter syndrome is to acknowledge and understand it. This means recognizing the patterns of self-doubt and negative self-talk that fuel the imposter phenomenon. It also means identifying the root causes of these feelings, whether they stem from childhood experiences, societal conditioning, or past failures.

Once you have a better understanding of your imposter syndrome, you can start to challenge the negative thoughts and beliefs that underlie it. This involves reframing your thinking, focusing on your strengths and accomplishments, and reminding yourself of your worth and value. It also means celebrating your successes, no matter how small they may seem.

Owning your accomplishments is a crucial part of overcoming imposter syndrome. This means acknowledging your hard work, dedication, and talent, and taking credit for your achievements. It also means recognizing that you are not an imposter, but a competent and capable individual who deserves to be where you are.

Building confidence is another key aspect of the journey from imposter syndrome to self-assurance. This can involve setting realistic goals, celebrating small wins, and practicing positive self-talk. It can also involve seeking support from mentors, coaches, or therapists who can help you develop a stronger sense of self-worth and overcome self-doubt.

It is important to remember that overcoming imposter syndrome is not a linear process. There will be setbacks and moments of doubt along the way. However, by consistently challenging negative thoughts, embracing your accomplishments, and building your confidence, you can gradually overcome imposter syndrome and embrace your full potential.

For women in male-dominated fields, overcoming imposter syndrome is not just about personal growth; it is also about breaking down barriers and creating a more inclusive workplace. By owning their accomplishments and advocating for themselves, women can challenge stereotypes and inspire others to do the same.

The journey from imposter syndrome to confidence is a transformative one. It is about shedding self-doubt and embracing self-belief. It is about recognizing your worth and owning your power. It is about stepping into your full potential and making your mark on the world. And for women in male-dominated fields, it is about breaking the mold, challenging the status quo, and creating a more equitable and inclusive future for all.

PPP

"She shed the cloak of self-doubt and embraced her brilliance."

With unwavering courage, she silenced the inner critic and owned her accomplishments, her journey a testament to the power of self-belief and the triumph over imposter syndrome. Her story is an anthem for women to rise above limitations and embrace their worth.

THIRTEEN

THE POWER OF COLLABORATION: WORKING WITH ALLIES TO DRIVE CHANGE

In the ongoing struggle for a more equitable and inclusive world, the power of collaboration cannot be underestimated. It is through the collective efforts of individuals, groups, and organizations working together that real and lasting change can be achieved. This is particularly true when it comes to advocating for women's rights and creating opportunities for them to thrive in traditionally male-dominated fields. The power of collaboration lies in its ability to amplify voices, pool resources, and create a united front that can effectively challenge systemic barriers and drive meaningful change.

One of the key benefits of collaboration is the amplification of voices. When individuals or groups come together, their collective voice becomes louder and more impactful. This is especially important for marginalized groups, whose voices are often silenced or ignored.

By working together, women can raise awareness of the challenges they face, advocate for their rights, and demand change. This collective voice can be a powerful force for change, influencing public opinion, policy decisions, and corporate practices.

Collaboration also enables the pooling of resources. Different individuals and organizations bring different strengths, skills, and resources to the table. By working together, they can leverage their collective resources to achieve goals that would be impossible to achieve alone.

This can include financial resources, expertise, networks, and influence. Pooling resources allows for a more comprehensive and effective approach to tackling complex issues such as gender inequality in the workplace.

Another powerful aspect of collaboration is the creation of a united front. When diverse individuals and organizations come together to work towards a common goal, they send a powerful message of solidarity and collective action. This united front can be a formidable force, challenging the status quo and pushing for change. It can also inspire others to join the movement, creating a ripple effect that can lead to widespread transformation.

Collaboration also fosters creativity and innovation. When people from different backgrounds and perspectives come together, they bring a diversity of ideas and approaches to the table. This can lead to new and innovative solutions to complex problems.

By working together, women can tap into their collective creativity and develop strategies that are more effective and sustainable.

Furthermore, collaboration can help to build trust and relationships between individuals and organizations. By working together towards a common goal, people develop a sense of shared purpose and mutual respect. This can lead to stronger and more sustainable partnerships, which are essential for driving long-term change.

However, collaboration is not without its challenges. It requires a willingness to compromise, to listen to different perspectives, and to work through disagreements.

It also requires a commitment to building trust and maintaining open communication. But the rewards of collaboration far outweigh the challenges. By working together, women can create a more equitable and inclusive world for themselves and for future generations.

The power of collaboration has been demonstrated time and again throughout history. From the suffragist movement to the civil rights movement to the fight for LGBTQ+ rights, collaboration has been a key driver of social change.

In the context of women's empowerment, collaboration has been instrumental in achieving milestones such as equal pay legislation, increased representation in leadership positions, and the creation of more inclusive workplace policies.

The power of collaboration is not limited to formal organizations or movements. It can also be found in informal networks of women who support and mentor each other. These networks can provide a safe space for women to share their experiences, seek advice, and find inspiration. They can also offer opportunities for professional development, networking, and advocacy.

In conclusion, the power of collaboration is a powerful tool for driving change and creating a more equitable and inclusive world. By working together, women can amplify their voices, pool their resources, and create a united front that can challenge systemic barriers and achieve their goals. Collaboration fosters creativity, innovation, and trust, and it is essential for building a more just and equitable society.

The journey towards gender equality is a long and ongoing one, but through collaboration, women can continue to make progress and create a better future for themselves and for generations to come.

ppp

"In collaboration, she found strength and forged a path towards change."

United with allies, she amplified her impact, her voice a chorus for progress. Her journey is a testament to the power of collective action and the transformative force of shared purpose.

FOURTEEN

RESILIENCE IN THE FACE OF ADVERSITY: TURNING CHALLENGES INTO OPPORTUNITIES

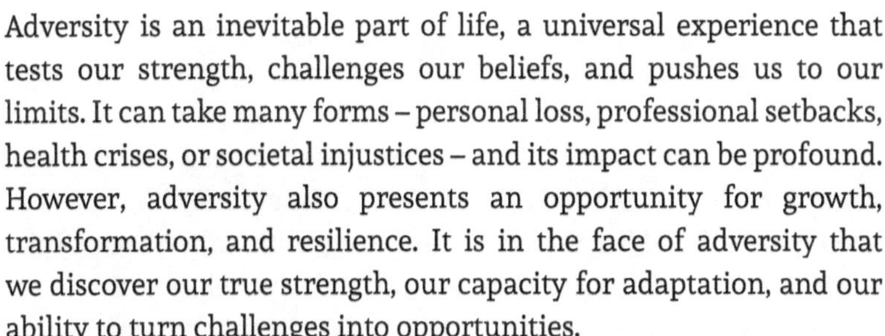

Adversity is an inevitable part of life, a universal experience that tests our strength, challenges our beliefs, and pushes us to our limits. It can take many forms – personal loss, professional setbacks, health crises, or societal injustices – and its impact can be profound. However, adversity also presents an opportunity for growth, transformation, and resilience. It is in the face of adversity that we discover our true strength, our capacity for adaptation, and our ability to turn challenges into opportunities.

Resilience, the ability to bounce back from adversity and thrive, is not an innate trait but a skill that can be developed and strengthened over time. It is a combination of internal factors, such as mindset, self-efficacy, and emotional regulation, and external factors, such as social support, resources, and opportunities. Resilience is not about avoiding or denying pain and difficulty; it is about acknowledging and processing them in a healthy way, learning from them, and using them as fuel for growth.

The journey to resilience begins with a shift in perspective. It requires reframing challenges as opportunities for learning and growth, rather than as insurmountable obstacles. It involves adopting a growth mindset, believing that we have the capacity to learn and develop, even in the face of adversity. This shift in perspective can empower us to approach challenges with curiosity and a willingness to experiment, rather than with fear and avoidance.

Another key aspect of resilience is the ability to regulate our emotions. Adversity can trigger a wide range of emotions, from anger and sadness to fear and anxiety. While it is important to acknowledge and process these emotions, it is equally important to avoid getting overwhelmed by them. Developing emotional regulation skills, such as mindfulness, meditation, and cognitive reappraisal, can help us manage our emotions in a healthy way, preventing them from derailing our progress.

Social support is another crucial factor in building resilience. Having a strong network of supportive relationships can provide us with the emotional and practical resources we need to cope with adversity. This can include family, friends, mentors, colleagues, or even professional therapists. Connecting with others who have faced similar challenges can be particularly helpful, as it can provide a sense of validation, understanding, and hope.

Resilience also involves learning from our experiences. Every challenge we face, every setback we encounter, is an opportunity to learn and grow. By reflecting on our experiences, identifying what worked and what didn't, and applying those lessons to future challenges, we can become more resilient over time.

Turning challenges into opportunities is not just about overcoming adversity; it is also about using those experiences to create something positive. This can involve using our newfound knowledge and skills to help others, advocating for change, or starting a new venture. By turning our pain into purpose, we can not only heal ourselves but also make a positive impact on the world.

The stories of individuals who have overcome adversity and achieved great things are a testament to the power of resilience. They demonstrate that even in the darkest of times, there is always hope, always a possibility for growth and transformation. They inspire us to embrace our challenges, to learn from our mistakes, and to never give up on our dreams.

Resilience is not a destination but a journey, a lifelong process of learning, adapting, and growing. It is about embracing the ups and downs of life, knowing that we have the strength and resources to navigate whatever comes our way. By cultivating resilience, we can not only survive adversity but thrive in the face of it, turning challenges into opportunities for growth, transformation, and positive impact.

ᐅᐅᐅ

"Adversity did not break her; it ignited her spirit."

With resilience as her armor, she transformed
challenges into opportunities, her journey a
testament to the indomitable human spirit. Her
story is a beacon of hope, illuminating the path
towards growth and transformation.

FIFTEEN

CREATING YOUR OWN PATH: DEFINING SUCCESS ON YOUR OWN TERMS

n the labyrinth of life, where paths are often predetermined and expectations loom large, the pursuit of personal success can become a convoluted journey. The conventional narrative often dictates a narrow definition of success, one that is often measured by external metrics such as wealth, fame, or societal recognition. However, true success lies not in conforming to these external standards, but in carving out your own unique path and defining success on your own terms.

This pursuit of self-defined success is particularly relevant for women navigating male-dominated fields. The traditional measures of success, often rooted in patriarchal norms and values, may not resonate with their individual aspirations and values. Moreover, these fields often present unique challenges for women, from implicit biases to systemic discrimination, making it even more crucial for them to chart their own course.

Creating your own path begins with introspection and self-awareness. It involves understanding your values, passions, and strengths. What truly motivates you? What are your unique talents and skills? What kind of impact do you want to make on the world? By answering these questions, you can start to articulate your own definition of success, one that aligns with your authentic self and aspirations.

This process of self-discovery is not always easy. It requires courage to challenge societal norms and expectations, to question the status quo, and to embrace your individuality. It may also involve unlearning deeply ingrained beliefs and values that no longer serve you. However, this journey of self-discovery is essential for creating a life that is truly fulfilling and meaningful.

Once you have a clear understanding of your values and aspirations, you can start to set goals that align with your definition of success. These goals may not be the same as the traditional markers of success, but they are the ones that matter most to you. They may involve making a difference in your community, pursuing a creative passion, or simply living a life of integrity and purpose.

Achieving these goals requires a combination of hard work, dedication, and resilience. It also requires a willingness to take risks, step outside of your comfort zone, and embrace failure as a learning opportunity. The path to success is rarely linear, and there will be setbacks and challenges along the way. However, by staying true to your values and your definition of success, you can navigate these challenges with grace and determination.

Creating your own path also involves surrounding yourself with supportive people who believe in you and your vision. This can include mentors, friends, family members, or colleagues who can offer guidance, encouragement, and a listening ear. It is also important to seek out role models who have carved out their own paths and achieved success on their own terms. Their stories can inspire and motivate you to keep moving forward, even when the going gets tough.

In addition to internal factors, creating your own path also involves navigating external challenges. This can include systemic barriers, such as discrimination and bias, that can hinder your progress. It is important to recognize these challenges and to develop strategies for overcoming them. This may involve advocating for yourself and others, building alliances with like-minded individuals, or seeking support from organizations that promote diversity and inclusion.

Ultimately, creating your own path is about taking ownership of your life and your career. It is about defining success on your own terms, rather than letting others dictate your path. It is about pursuing your passions, living authentically, and making a positive impact on the world. By embracing this mindset, you can create a life that is truly fulfilling and meaningful, one that reflects your unique values and aspirations.

Creating your own path is not a selfish act; it is a powerful act of self-empowerment. By defining success on your own terms, you not only create a more fulfilling life for yourself but also inspire others to do the same. You become a role model for those who are seeking to break free from societal expectations and chart their own course. Your journey becomes a beacon of hope, showing others that it is possible to create a life that is truly meaningful, regardless of what society dictates.

ᕴᕴᕴ

"She didn't follow the well-trodden path; she created her own."

With unwavering determination, she defied expectations and charted a course that resonated with her soul. Her journey is a testament to the power of authenticity and the freedom to define success on one's own terms.

SIXTEEN

CELEBRATING DIVERSITY: EMBRACING DIFFERENT PERSPECTIVES AND EXPERIENCES

In the intricate tapestry of human existence, diversity is not merely a buzzword or a corporate initiative; it is the essence of our collective identity. It encompasses the vast spectrum of human experiences, perspectives, backgrounds, and identities that make us unique. Embracing diversity is not just about acknowledging these differences; it is about celebrating them, valuing them, and integrating them into every aspect of our lives. It is about creating a world where everyone feels seen, heard, and empowered to contribute their unique talents and perspectives.

Diversity is not a monolith; it encompasses a multitude of

dimensions. It includes race, ethnicity, gender, sexual orientation, age, disability, religion, socioeconomic status, and countless other characteristics that shape our identities and experiences. Each of these dimensions adds a layer of richness and complexity to our world, offering a kaleidoscope of perspectives that can enrich our understanding of ourselves and others.

Embracing diversity starts with recognizing the value of different perspectives and experiences. It means acknowledging that our own worldview is limited, shaped by our own unique experiences and biases. By actively seeking out and engaging with different perspectives, we can broaden our understanding of the world and challenge our own assumptions. This can lead to greater empathy, compassion, and understanding, fostering a more inclusive and equitable society.

Celebrating diversity also means recognizing the unique contributions that individuals from different backgrounds bring to the table. Each person's experiences, skills, and knowledge are shaped by their unique identity, and these diverse perspectives can lead to innovative solutions, creative ideas, and a more robust understanding of complex issues. By valuing and incorporating diverse perspectives into decision-making processes, we can create more effective and equitable outcomes for everyone.

Embracing diversity is not just about individual actions; it is also about creating systemic change. This means challenging and dismantling the structures and systems that perpetuate inequality and discrimination. It means advocating for policies and practices that promote diversity and inclusion in all aspects of society, from education and employment to healthcare and housing.

In the workplace, embracing diversity can lead to numerous benefits. Studies have shown that diverse teams are more innovative, creative, and productive. They are better at problem-solving, decision-making, and adapting to change. By fostering a culture of diversity and inclusion, organizations can tap into the full potential of their workforce, leading to greater success and innovation.

In education, embracing diversity can enrich the learning experience for all students. By exposing students to different cultures, perspectives, and ways of thinking, educators can foster critical thinking, cultural competence, and a more nuanced understanding of the world. This can prepare students to thrive in an increasingly diverse and interconnected global society.

In our communities, embracing diversity can create a more vibrant and welcoming environment for everyone. By celebrating our differences and finding common ground, we can build stronger relationships, foster greater understanding, and create a more inclusive society where everyone feels a sense of belonging.

The journey to embrace diversity is ongoing and requires continuous effort and commitment. It involves challenging our own biases, educating ourselves about different cultures and perspectives, and actively seeking out opportunities to engage with people from different backgrounds. It also involves advocating for systemic change and creating a more inclusive environment for everyone.

The benefits of embracing diversity are immeasurable. It can lead to greater innovation, creativity, and understanding. It can foster stronger relationships, build more resilient communities, and create a more equitable and just society. By embracing diversity, we not only celebrate our differences but also recognize our shared humanity, creating a world where everyone can thrive.

ᐅᐅᐅ

"She didn't just embrace diversity; she celebrated it as a symphony of human experience."

Recognizing the richness of different perspectives, she fostered an inclusive environment where every voice mattered. Her leadership is a testament to the power of unity in diversity and the beauty of a world where everyone belongs.

SEVENTEEN

THE FUTURE IS FEMALE: VISIONS FOR A MORE EQUITABLE WORLD

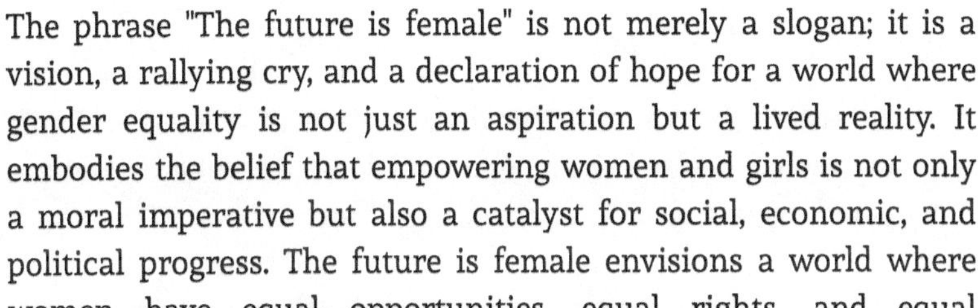

The phrase "The future is female" is not merely a slogan; it is a vision, a rallying cry, and a declaration of hope for a world where gender equality is not just an aspiration but a lived reality. It embodies the belief that empowering women and girls is not only a moral imperative but also a catalyst for social, economic, and political progress. The future is female envisions a world where women have equal opportunities, equal rights, and equal representation in all spheres of life.

This vision of a more equitable world is rooted in the understanding that gender equality is not just about women; it is about creating a better world for everyone. When women are empowered, they invest in their families, communities, and economies.

They are more likely to educate their children, promote health and well-being, and advocate for social justice. Empowering women is, therefore, a key driver of sustainable development and a more equitable world.

A future where women lead is one where diverse perspectives and experiences shape decision-making at all levels. Studies have shown that organizations with gender-diverse leadership teams are more innovative, profitable, and sustainable.

They are also better equipped to address complex challenges and make decisions that reflect the needs of a diverse population. In politics, women leaders have been shown to prioritize issues such as education, healthcare, and social welfare, leading to more equitable and inclusive policies.

This vision also encompasses a world where women are free from violence and discrimination. Gender-based violence is a global pandemic that affects millions of women and girls worldwide. It not only violates their human rights but also has devastating consequences for their physical and mental health, economic well-being, and overall quality of life.

A future where the future is female is one where women and girls can live their lives free from fear and violence, where they are valued and respected as equal members of society.

Furthermore, this vision entails a world where women have equal access to education, healthcare, and economic opportunities. Education is a fundamental human right and a key driver of empowerment. When girls are educated, they are more likely to delay marriage and childbirth, earn higher incomes, and participate in decision-making.

Similarly, access to healthcare is essential for women's well-being and empowerment. This includes not only reproductive healthcare but also access to comprehensive health services that address the unique needs of women throughout their lives.

Economic empowerment is another critical aspect of this vision. When women have equal access to economic opportunities, they can contribute to their families, communities, and economies.

This means ensuring that women have equal access to education and training, financial services, and markets. It also means addressing discriminatory practices that limit women's economic participation, such as unequal pay, lack of access to credit, and barriers to entrepreneurship.

The future is female also envisions a world where women's voices are heard and valued in all spheres of life. This means ensuring that women have equal representation in decision-making bodies, from local councils to national parliaments to international organizations. It also means creating a culture where women's perspectives are respected and their contributions are valued.

To achieve this vision of a more equitable world, we need to take a multifaceted approach. This includes investing in girls' education, empowering women economically, promoting women's health and well-being, addressing gender-based violence, and advocating for policies and practices that promote gender equality. It also involves changing societal attitudes and norms that perpetuate gender stereotypes and discrimination.

The journey towards a more equitable world is a long and ongoing one, but the progress made so far is encouraging. More and more women are breaking barriers, shattering glass ceilings, and achieving leadership positions in various fields.

Their stories serve as an inspiration and a reminder that the future is indeed female. By continuing to invest in women and girls, we can create a world where everyone has the opportunity to thrive, regardless of their gender.

The future is female is not just a slogan; it is a call to action. It is a vision of a world where women are empowered, respected, and valued as equal partners in shaping a more just, equitable, and sustainable future for all. It is a future that we must all work towards, together.

ᏜᏜᏜ

"The future is not just female; it's a harmonious blend of voices, united in purpose."

Her vision transcended gender, embracing a world where equality reigns and everyone has the opportunity to thrive. Her legacy is a commitment to building a more just and equitable world, one where the future belongs to all.

EIGHTEEN

UNLEASHING YOUR POTENTIAL: OVERCOMING SELF-DOUBT AND FEAR

Self-doubt and fear are universal human experiences, lurking in the shadows of our minds and threatening to sabotage our dreams and aspirations. They can be paralyzing, preventing us from taking risks, pursuing our goals, and reaching our full potential. However, these internal barriers are not insurmountable. By acknowledging their presence, understanding their origins, and developing strategies to overcome them, we can unleash our potential and live a life of purpose, passion, and fulfillment.

Self-doubt is the nagging voice in our heads that questions our abilities, worth, and potential. It tells us we're not good enough, smart enough, or capable enough to achieve our goals. It can stem from past experiences, negative self-talk, or comparison to others.

Self-doubt can erode our confidence, dampen our motivation, and hold us back from taking action.

Fear, on the other hand, is a natural human response to perceived threats or dangers. It can manifest as anxiety, worry, or even panic. Fear can protect us from harm, but it can also hold us back from pursuing our dreams. Fear of failure, rejection, or the unknown can keep us trapped in our comfort zones, preventing us from taking the necessary risks to grow and evolve.

The first step in overcoming self-doubt and fear is to acknowledge their presence. We often try to ignore or suppress these feelings, but this only serves to amplify them. By acknowledging our doubts and fears, we can begin to understand them and develop strategies to manage them.

Understanding the origins of our self-doubt and fear is crucial. Often, these feelings stem from past experiences, negative self-talk, or societal expectations. By exploring these root causes, we can gain insights into why we feel the way we do and develop more effective strategies for overcoming them.

One effective strategy for overcoming self-doubt is to challenge negative self-talk. When you catch yourself thinking negative thoughts about yourself, ask yourself if they are based on facts or assumptions. Are you being overly critical of yourself? Are you comparing yourself to others unfairly? By challenging negative self-talk and replacing it with positive affirmations, you can gradually build your confidence and self-belief.

Another strategy is to focus on your strengths and accomplishments. Make a list of your achievements, big and small. Remind yourself of the challenges you have overcome and the obstacles you have conquered. By focusing on your strengths and accomplishments, you can shift your perspective from self-doubt to self-appreciation.

Building resilience is also crucial for overcoming fear. Resilience is the ability to bounce back from setbacks, learn from failures, and keep moving forward. It involves developing a growth mindset, believing that you can learn and grow from your experiences, even the difficult ones. By building resilience, you can develop the courage to face your fears and take the necessary risks to achieve your goals.

Taking action is another key strategy for overcoming self-doubt and fear. When we feel overwhelmed by these feelings, it is easy to become paralyzed and avoid taking action. However, taking small steps towards our goals can help us build momentum and confidence. By breaking down our goals into smaller, more manageable tasks, we can make progress and overcome our fears.

Surrounding yourself with supportive people is also essential. Seek out mentors, coaches, friends, and family members who believe in you and encourage you to pursue your dreams. Their support and encouragement can be invaluable in overcoming self-doubt and fear.

Additionally, practicing self-compassion is crucial. We are often our own harshest critics, holding ourselves to unrealistic standards and berating ourselves for our mistakes. Self-compassion involves treating ourselves with kindness and understanding, acknowledging our imperfections, and forgiving ourselves for our mistakes. By practicing self-compassion, we can create a more supportive and nurturing internal environment that fosters growth and resilience.

Unleashing our potential is not about eliminating self-doubt and fear altogether. These feelings are a natural part of the human experience. However, by acknowledging them, understanding their origins, and developing strategies to manage them, we can prevent them from holding us back. By embracing our imperfections, celebrating our strengths, and taking bold action towards our goals, we can unlock our full potential and create a life that is both meaningful and fulfilling. Remember, the journey to unleashing your potential is not a destination but an ongoing process. It requires continuous self-reflection, growth, and resilience. But the rewards are immeasurable. By overcoming self-doubt and fear, you can live a life that is true to your values, passions, and dreams.

"She unleashed her potential, not by conquering fear, but by dancing with it."

Embracing vulnerability as a strength, she transformed her doubts into fuel for growth. Her journey is a testament to the power of self-acceptance and the courage to step into the unknown.

NINETEEN

Leading with Authenticity: Staying True to Your Values

In a world often characterized by conformity and the pressure to fit in, leading with authenticity stands as a beacon of true leadership. Authenticity is the alignment of our inner values, beliefs, and actions. It is about being genuine, transparent, and true to oneself, even when faced with challenges or pressures to conform. For women in leadership roles, particularly those in male-dominated fields, leading with authenticity can be a powerful tool for personal and organizational success.

Authenticity in leadership is not about being perfect or having all the answers. It is about recognizing and embracing one's strengths and weaknesses, acknowledging mistakes, and learning from them. It is about being open and transparent in communication, building trust and rapport with others, and inspiring them through genuine connection and shared purpose.

One of the fundamental aspects of authentic leadership is self-awareness. Leaders who are in tune with their values, beliefs, and emotions are better equipped to make decisions that align with their true selves. They are also more likely to inspire trust and respect from others, as their actions are consistent with their words. This self-awareness allows them to lead with integrity and authenticity, even when faced with difficult choices or conflicting priorities.

Leading with authenticity also involves being vulnerable. This does not mean oversharing personal details or weaknesses, but rather acknowledging one's limitations and being open to feedback. Vulnerability can foster a culture of trust and openness within a team, encouraging others to share their own vulnerabilities and challenges. This can lead to greater collaboration, innovation, and ultimately, better outcomes.

Authentic leaders are also values-driven. They have a clear understanding of their core values and principles, and they use these as a compass to guide their decisions and actions. They are not afraid to stand up for what they believe in, even when it is unpopular or inconvenient. This commitment to values inspires others and creates a sense of purpose and meaning within the organization.

In male-dominated fields, women leaders often face unique challenges. They may feel pressure to conform to masculine norms or to downplay their femininity. However, authentic leadership allows women to embrace their unique strengths and perspectives, leading to a more inclusive and diverse leadership style. By staying true to their values and embracing their authentic selves, women leaders can inspire others, challenge stereotypes, and create a more equitable workplace.

Authenticity also fosters a sense of psychological safety within a team. When leaders are open and honest about their own struggles and challenges, it creates a space where others feel safe to do the same. This can lead to increased trust, collaboration, and innovation, as team members feel empowered to share their ideas and take risks without fear of judgment or retribution.

Leading with authenticity is not always easy. It requires courage, self-reflection, and a willingness to be vulnerable. However, the rewards are immense. Authentic leaders inspire trust, loyalty, and commitment from their teams. They create a culture of openness, collaboration, and innovation. And they are more likely to achieve sustainable success, as their actions are aligned with their values and their true selves.

In a world that is constantly changing and evolving, authenticity is a timeless leadership quality. It is a quality that transcends gender, race, and background. It is a quality that resonates with people on a deep level, inspiring them to be their best selves and to work together towards a common goal.

For women in leadership roles, authenticity is not just a choice; it is a necessity. By staying true to their values and embracing their unique strengths, women leaders can break down barriers, challenge stereotypes, and create a more inclusive and equitable future for all. The future is not just female; it is authentic.

ᎮᎮᎮ

"Authenticity was her compass, guiding her through the labyrinth of leadership."

With unwavering integrity, she led with her heart, inspiring others to follow suit. Her journey is a testament to the power of leading with truth and the transformative impact of genuine connection.

TWENTY

BEYOND BARRIERS: A BLUEPRINT FOR WOMEN'S SUCCESS IN ANY FIELD

In the ever-evolving landscape of the 21st century, women are shattering glass ceilings and breaking barriers across various fields. While progress has been made, the journey towards true gender equality is far from over. "Beyond Barriers" is a blueprint for women's success, a guide to navigating challenges and unlocking their full potential in any chosen field. It is a testament to women's resilience, determination, and unwavering spirit in the face of adversity.

At the core of this blueprint lies the fundamental principle of self-belief. Women must believe in their abilities, their worth, and their potential to achieve greatness. This involves challenging societal norms and expectations, overcoming internalized biases, and embracing their unique strengths and perspectives. It is about recognizing that their gender is not a limitation but a source of power and resilience.

Education and skill development are critical components of this blueprint. Women need to invest in their education and continuously update their skills to stay competitive in the ever-changing job market. This involves pursuing higher education, attending workshops and conferences, and seeking mentorship from experienced professionals. By investing in their knowledge and skills, women can enhance their expertise, increase their confidence, and open doors to new opportunities.

Networking and building relationships are also essential for women's success. Building a strong network of mentors, peers, and allies can provide invaluable support, guidance, and opportunities. It is important for women to connect with other women in their field, as well as with male allies who are committed to gender equality. These relationships can offer a safe space for sharing experiences, seeking advice, and building a community of support.

Advocacy and self-promotion are equally important. Women need to be their own champions, speaking up for their accomplishments and advocating for their needs and aspirations. This involves negotiating for fair compensation, seeking promotions, and asking for what they deserve. It also means celebrating their successes and sharing their stories to inspire and empower other women.

Navigating workplace challenges is another critical aspect of this blueprint. Women often face unique challenges in the workplace, such as unconscious bias, microaggressions, and the "double bind" of being seen as either too assertive or too passive. By developing strategies to address these challenges, such as assertiveness training, negotiation skills, and conflict resolution, women can create a more inclusive and supportive work environment for themselves and others.

Work-life balance is also a crucial consideration. Women often bear the brunt of caregiving responsibilities, which can make it challenging to balance their professional and personal lives. However, by setting boundaries, prioritizing self-care, and seeking support from partners, family, and friends, women can achieve a more harmonious balance between their work and personal lives.

Resilience and perseverance are essential qualities for women navigating any field. Setbacks and failures are inevitable, but it is important to view them as learning opportunities rather than roadblocks. By cultivating resilience, women can bounce back from adversity, learn from their mistakes, and continue to pursue their goals with renewed determination.

The blueprint for women's success is not a one-size-fits-all solution. It is a dynamic and evolving framework that needs to be adapted to individual circumstances and goals. However, the principles outlined above provide a solid foundation for women to build upon as they navigate their chosen paths.

By embracing self-belief, investing in education and skill development, building strong networks, advocating for themselves, navigating workplace challenges, prioritizing work-life balance, and cultivating resilience, women can unleash their full potential and achieve success in any field. The future is bright for women who are willing to break barriers, challenge the status quo, and create their own paths to success. It is a future where women are not just equal but empowered to lead and make a lasting impact on the world.

ppp

"Beyond barriers, she soared, a testament to the limitless potential within every woman."

With resilience, determination, and unwavering self-belief, she defied expectations and achieved the impossible. Her journey is an inspiration to all who dare to dream big, to break free from limitations, and to create a life that is truly their own.

TWENTY-ONE
SUMMARY

"Beyond Barriers: Women Thriving in Male-Dominated Fields" is a testament to women's resilience, determination, and unwavering spirit in the face of adversity. The book delves into the multifaceted journey of women who have not only dared to enter traditionally male-dominated fields but have also excelled in them. This summary chapter aims to encapsulate the key lessons and insights presented in the book, offering a blueprint for women's success in any field.

The book begins by acknowledging the trailblazing women who paved the way for future generations. These pioneers shattered glass ceilings, defied expectations, and challenged gender stereotypes, proving that women are capable of achieving greatness in any field. Their stories of resilience and determination serve as a powerful inspiration for aspiring women leaders.

Building on this foundation, the book explores the various challenges women face in male-dominated fields, from navigating bias and discrimination to juggling career and personal life. It offers practical strategies for overcoming these challenges, such as building strong networks, finding your voice, and advocating for yourself. It emphasizes the importance of mentorship and role models, highlighting the power of female leaders who can guide and inspire younger women.

The book also delves into the importance of personal development and empowerment. It emphasizes the need for women to own their accomplishments, overcome self-doubt, and unleash their full potential. It also stresses the significance of staying true to one's values, leading with authenticity, and embracing diversity as a source of strength.

Creating a more inclusive workplace is another key theme of the book. It outlines strategies for changing the game, including challenging gender stereotypes, promoting diversity and inclusion, and fostering a culture of respect and equity. It emphasizes the power of collaboration, highlighting the importance of working with allies to drive change and create a more equitable world for all.

The book concludes by offering a comprehensive blueprint for women's success in any field. This blueprint encompasses a range of strategies, from investing in education and skill development to building strong networks and advocating for oneself. It emphasizes the importance of resilience, perseverance, and a strong belief in one's abilities. It also highlights the need for work-life balance, self-care, and continuous learning.

Ultimately, "Beyond Barriers" is a call to action for women everywhere. It is a reminder that women are capable of achieving anything they set their minds to, regardless of the challenges they may face. It is a celebration of women's achievements and a roadmap for future success. By embracing the lessons and insights presented in this book, women can break down barriers, shatter glass ceilings, and create a more equitable and inclusive world for themselves and for generations to come.

The book serves as a reminder that the future is female. By empowering young women to lead, celebrating diversity, and creating a more equitable world, we can unlock the full potential of humanity and build a brighter future for all. This is not just a vision; it is a call to action for everyone who believes in a world where women are not only equal but empowered to lead and make a lasting impact on the world.

❦❦❦

Citation And References

This book represents the culmination of extensive research and meticulous analysis, incorporating a diverse range of sources, including numerous books, scholarly studies, and personal experiences. Additionally, I have scoured various websites to gather relevant information and data essential for the compilation of this work. I have taken every precaution to ensure the accuracy of the information presented and have diligently cited all sources to acknowledge their contributions.

Despite these efforts, the possibility of inadvertent errors remains. I deeply value the insights of my readers and appreciate any feedback that can help identify and rectify such inaccuracies. I encourage you to bring any discrepancies to my attention.

Your feedback is not only welcome but crucial, as it will aid in correcting current editions and enhancing the content of future ones. I am committed to maintaining the highest standards of accuracy and reliability in my work and thank you for your support and understanding.

Additionally, I firmly uphold the principle of freedom of speech and expression as guaranteed under Article 19(1)(a) of the Constitution of India, and I respect the diverse viewpoints and expressions of all readers.

ᐅᐅᐅ

Other Books Of The Author

1. Empowering Minds: A Journey into Women's Self-Discovery and Power
2. The Dynamics of Motivation: Catalyzing Thought into Action
3. Meditation and Mental Well Being: The Path to Inner Peace and Clarity
4. The Psychology of Child Education: Nurturing Future Generations
5. Ethical Enlightenment: A Modern Guide to Living with Integrity
6. Voices of Empowerment: Stories of Women Rising Against Odds
7. Social Psychology in Everyday Life: Understanding Human Connections
8. The Essence of Motivational Speaking: Inspiring Change in Others
9. Balancing Acts: Women, Work, and the Will to Lead
10. Guiding with Grace: Raising Children with Compassion and Awareness
11. The Power of Positive Aging: Embracing Life After Fifty
12. Building Resilient Communities: Social Work in Action
13. The Ethical Educator: Principles for Teaching and Learning
14. From Insight to Impact: Social Psychology for a Better World
15. The Ethics of Empathy: A Guide to Ethical Living
16. The Science of Empowering the Self: Navigating Life's Challenges with Psychological Wisdom
17. The Mindful Conscious Leader: Meditation Techniques for Modern Management
18. Pioneering Spirit: Women's Pathways to Leadership and Empowerment
19. Feeling to Healing: The Role of Emotional Intelligence in Child Development
20. Transformative Talks and Words of Inspiration: Insights into Motivational Oratory

72. The Resilience Factor: Transforming Setbacks into Stepping Stones
73. The Healing Touch of Nature: An Introduction to Naturopathy
74. Echoes of the Past: Healing Through Past Life Regression
75. The Spiritual Healer's Handbook: Exploring Energy Medicine
76. Crystal Clarity: Unveiling the Power of Gemstones
77. The Dream Weaver's Guide: Decoding the Language of Dreams
78. Emotional Alchemy: Transforming Pain into Power
79. Sonic Serenity: Harnessing Sound for Stress Relief
80. The Entrepreneur's Playbook: Launching Your Business with Confidence
81. Productivity Unleashed: Time Management Strategies for Entrepreneurs
82. The Problem Solver's Toolkit: Creative Solutions for Business Challenges
83. The Future is Now: Emerging Trends in Business
84. The Curious Explorer: A Child's Guide to Scientific Discovery
85. Digital Pioneers: Empowering Kids in the Tech World
86. The Young Philosopher's Guide: Exploring Life's Big Questions
87. Finding Your Voice: Communication Skills for Confident Kids
88. Nature's Playground: A Child's Guide to Outdoor Adventure
89. Growing a Greener Tomorrow: A Guide to Tree Planting & Conservation
90. Driving with Purpose: Ethical Choices on the Road
91. The Healing Touch: Cultivating Compassion in Healthcare
92. Navigating the Digital Landscape: Ethics in the Age of Social Media
93. The Ethical Closet: A Guide to Sustainable Fashion
94. The Mindful Voyager: Sustainable Travel Practices
95. The Feminine Divine: Honoring the Goddesses of India
96. Sacred Sounds: Chanting Your Way to Inner Peace
97. The Yoga Path: Uniting with the Divine Within
98. Rites of Passage: Creating Meaningful Ceremonies
99. The Chakra System: A Map of Inner Transformation
100. Spiritual Sangha: Finding Community through Satsang and

Bhajan

101. Pilgrimage of the Soul: Spiritual Journeys in India

❧❧❧

Contact

Dr. Minakshi Bansal
Social Activist
Ahmedabad, Gujarat, Bharat
minakshiindiag20@yahoo.com

ᘓᘓᘓ

|| LOKAHA SAMASTHAHA SUKHINO BHAVANTU ||